1-10-2021 FB

P̲ositive thinking is a habit... we can practice it every day until it becomes second nature to us — and along the way, transform our lives.

Washington L. Crowley

Blue Mountain Arts®

New and Best-Selling Titles

By Susan Polis Schutz:

*To My Daughter with Love
on the Important Things in Life*

To My Grandchild with Love

To My Son with Love

～

By Douglas Pagels:

*Always Remember How Special
You Are to Me*

For You, My Soul Mate

The Next Chapter of Your Life

Required Reading for All Teenagers

*Simple Thoughts That Can Literally
Change Your Life*

You Are One Amazing Lady

～

By Wally Amos, with Stu Glauberman:

*The Path to Success Is Paved
with Positive Thinking*

～

By Minx Boren:

Friendship Is a Journey

Healing Is a Journey

By Marci:

Angels Are Everywhere!

Friends Are Forever

10 Simple Things to Remember

To My Daughter

To My Granddaughter

To My Mother

To My Sister

To My Son

You Are My "Once in a Lifetime"

～

By Debra DiPietro:

Short Morning Prayers

～

By Carol Wiseman:

Emerging from the Heartache of Loss

～

By Latesha Randall:

The To-Be List

～

By Dr. Preston C. VanLoon:

The Path to Forgiveness

Anthologies:

A Daybook of Positive Thinking

Dream Big, Stay Positive, and Believe in Yourself

God Is Always Watching Over You

Hang In There

The Love Between a Mother and Daughter Is Forever

Nothing Fills the Heart with Joy like a Grandson

A Son Is Life's Greatest Gift

There Is Nothing Sweeter in Life Than a Granddaughter

There Is So Much to Love About You… Daughter

Think Positive Thoughts Every Day

Words Every Woman Should Remember

You Are Stronger Than You Know

Think
Positive
Thoughts
Every Day

Words to Inspire
a Brighter Outlook
on Life

Edited by Patricia Wayant

Blue Mountain Press™
Boulder, Colorado

We wish to thank Susan Polis Schutz for permission to reprint the following poems that appear in this publication: "Find Happiness in Everything You Do" and "Be a Positive Thinker." Copyright © 1983, 1986 by Stephen Schutz and Susan Polis Schutz. And for "This life is yours." Copyright © 1979 by Continental Publications. All rights reserved.

Library of Congress Control Number: 2011911702
ISBN: 978-1-68088-250-6 (previously ISBN: 978-1-59842-623-6)

◾ and Blue Mountain Press are registered in U.S. Patent and Trademark Office.
Certain trademarks are used under license.

Printed in China.
First printing of this edition: 2018

✿ This book is printed on recycled paper.

This book is printed on paper that has been specially produced to be acid free (neutral pH) and contains no groundwood or unbleached pulp. It conforms with the requirements of the American National Standards Institute, Inc., so as to ensure that this book will last and be enjoyed by future generations.

Blue Mountain Arts, Inc.
P.O. Box 4549, Boulder, Colorado 80306

Contents

1-12-21 7B

Think Positive Thoughts Every Day ✓

Take a moment to look around and smile at your life and your choices. Don't worry about the paths you should have taken or the opportunities you ignored. Instead, breathe in the life that surrounds you — let it fill your soul with light and hope.

Reflect on the past and all the memories, good and bad, that have made you who you are today. Your journey is far from over, as you will continue to grow, change, and flourish.

Life can be so busy, and we sometimes take for granted the important little things that make us smile. Look at the sunset, share a cup of coffee with your best friend, or hear the wind rustle through the trees. Take some time to listen to life and feel the sun on your face, and stop to watch butterflies in your garden.

Take a moment every day to think positive thoughts.

Carol Schelling

Don't Let Anything Steal Your Joy

Choose to be well in every way. Choose to be happy no matter what. Decide that each day will be good just because you're alive.

You have power over your thoughts and feelings. Don't let your circumstances dictate how you feel. Don't let your thoughts and feelings color your situation blue or desperate.

Even if you don't have everything you want, even if you're in pain or in need, you can choose to be joyful no matter what you're experiencing. You are more than your body, your physical presence, and your material possessions. You are spirit. You have your mind, heart, and soul, and there is always something to be thankful for. 7B 11/15/21

Decide that life is good and you are special. Decide to enjoy today. Decide that you will live life to the fullest now, no matter what. Trust that you will change what needs changing, but also decide that you're not going to put off enjoying life just because you don't have everything you want now. Steadfastly refuse to let anything steal your joy. Choose to be happy... and you will be!

Donna Fargo

Be a Positive Thinker ✓

Have confidence in yourself
Have a very strong sense of purpose
Never have excuses for not doing something
Always try your hardest for perfection
Never consider the idea of failing
Work extremely hard toward your goals
Know who you are
Understand your weaknesses
    as well as your strong points
Accept and benefit from criticism
Know when to defend what you are doing
Be creative
Do not be afraid to be a little different
    in finding innovative solutions that
        will enable you to achieve your dreams

≈

Susan Polis Schutz

You've Got Choices √

When you have something particularly challenging to deal with, try to remind yourself...

You've got this moment... You can choose to be happy or unhappy. You can choose what you think, what you say, and how you feel. You can choose to be hopeful or hopeless, to respond angrily or cheerfully, to be bored or interested.

You've got this day... No matter what the weather is like, you can choose what kind of day it will be — beautiful or awful or somewhere in between. You can choose what you will do and what you won't — to give up or give in or go on. You have a choice to do something or nothing, to start now or later. You can choose your attitude about what you're facing.

You've got your life... If you're not happy, satisfied, encouraged, and hopeful, you're cheating yourself. You can talk and talk to yourself about what you need to do to honor your life, but if you don't turn those thoughts into actions, you're just playing games and giving up to whatever comes to mind.

You've got the power to make choices... Your life is the manifestation of the choices you make each moment and each day. When you use this awesome gift to your best advantage, there is nothing you can't do.

Donna Fargo

Look on the Bright Side√

Think about the good things in life, like sunshine, holidays, feeling loved, special friendships, and laughter. Think about rainbows, blue skies, and beautiful sunsets and feel loved, cared about, and accepted. Remember that in life, although there is some bad stuff, good things really do happen, too.

Maria Mullins

Change Your Thoughts...
Change Your Life

I am convinced that attitude is the key
to success or failure in almost any of life's
endeavors. Your attitude — your perspective,
your outlook, how you feel about yourself,
how you feel about other people — determines
your priorities, your actions, your values. Your
attitude determines how you interact with other
people and how you interact with yourself.

Caroline Warner

When you say to yourself, "I am going to have a pleasant visit or a pleasant journey," you are literally sending elements and forces ahead of your body that will arrange things to make your visit or journey pleasant. When before the visit or the journey or the shopping trip you are in a bad humor, or fearful or apprehensive of something unpleasant, you are sending unseen agencies ahead of you, which will make some kind of unpleasantness. Our thoughts, or in other words, our state of mind, is ever at work "fixing up" things good or bad in advance.

Prentice Mulford

You Don't Have to Accept Defeat

Sometimes life just throws us a curve,
and we're often so taken by surprise
that we feel helpless.
We forget how capable we are;
we forget how to summon our strength,
square our shoulders,
and find hope.
When the unexpected happens,
it's good to remember
that you don't have to accept defeat
or bow to circumstances.
You just need to call on
that courageous spirit within you,
let your confidence shine through,
and remember how capable you are.

Sometimes it helps to be reminded
of those qualities that
keep you strong and moving forward.
Remember those other times
that tried to get you down
but didn't stand a chance
because you are strong and capable
and a winner through and through!

— Barbara J. Hall

We Can't Control the Outer World, but We Can Master the One Within

We can't always control the
people, events, or circumstances
that surround us,
but we can control the way we choose
to react to them. ✓ 9/13/11
No person or thing has the power
to make us angry or scared or frustrated —
these are simply ways we choose to respond.
Instead of feeling resentful that people
don't always act the way we'd like
or circumstances don't always unfold
as we'd prefer,
it helps to focus instead
on our inner beings —
on becoming more aware
of the thoughts and feelings
we want to experience.

When we no longer rely on
circumstances
to make us happy
and choose happiness in spite of them,
we soon notice the very things we
found objectionable
magically fading away.
And in their place cascades
a glorious deluge of all things
deserving and reflective
of our good energy.

We can't always control
the world around us,
but we can master the one within
and create joy and beauty
both inside and out.

Lynn Keachie

Don't Lose Faith
in Yourself

Trust your decisions and feelings
and do what is best for you.
The future will work itself out.
Don't let anyone else's negativity
influence your dreams, values,
  or hopes.
Focus on what you can change
and let go of what you can't.
You know your own worth,
what you've accomplished,
and what you're capable of.
Your goals may take a bit longer
and be harder to achieve
than you had hoped, but...

Concentrate on the positives
and combine faith with
generous portions of patience
and determination.
Step boldly and confidently
    into your future
where happiness, success,
and dreams await you.

Barbara Cage

You Can Rise Above Anything

Sometimes, it seems as if
the world around you
is spinning out of control.
Thankfully, the very things
that can help you through
times like these
are the ones you have
complete control over.

Faith... hope... heart...
these are the things
that keep you empowered.
They can't be taken from you,
but you can use them
to face adversity head on
and rise triumphantly above it.

No matter what unfolds,
remember that nothing
has the power
to pull you
into a downward spiral.
Instead, you can use
any difficulty you encounter
as a springboard
to send you soaring
among the stars.

Lynn Keachie

Keep Moving Forward

Do not allow past shortcomings
to govern who you are now —
everyone falls short sometimes.

✓ 1/19/22

Do not allow previous misfortunes
to dictate who you will become —
everyone can change.

On your path to self-discovery,
there's a bridge
between who you were
and who you want to be.

One step at a time,
walk this crossing.
There's no need to run,
because a reflective journey
takes time.

Simply move forward,
face full to the sun,
and see yourself
for who you want to be.

Become a better you,
empowered and emancipated
from all that was holding you back.

Angela Rene Goughnour

Try Not to Worry

Worry will distract you
from the treasures ahead.
Instead, keep love and happiness
in your heart.
Lift your spirits and stay alert
to the gifts around you.
Don't waste your time wondering
what others may think.
You are the only one
who has walked in your shoes.
You are the most qualified
to decide what path you will take.

Fill your journey with
love and harmony,
joy and bliss.
Look at the world
through the eyes of a child,
and carry your memories
in a heart filled with love
and peace.

Christina Curtis

Learn from Your Mistakes

Consider each disappointment and trouble as so much experience and as a temporary lesson set for you to learn.

Ella Wheeler Wilcox

The only real mistake we make is the one from which we learn nothing.

John Wesley Powell

Setbacks and disappointments are something we all experience at one time or another. But if you refuse to believe in failure, you'll be able to find a way to open up all those doors that at one time you thought were closed to you forever. If you mark something down as a failure, then that's what it will be. But if you make up your mind to get the better of the situation, an experience that you once labeled as a failure can become another steppingstone toward happiness. So the next time something doesn't turn out exactly as you'd hoped, turn it around, be a fighter. Remember: it's the people who can turn a negative into a positive and bounce back who really get ahead in life.

≈

Mary Lou Retton

As Long as You Have Hope, All Things Are Possible

Hope is found in the way
you look at life.
It's the path you're drawn
to follow.
It's in the plans you must arrange,
the goals you want to reach,
the dream that takes
your breath away.

Hope is there when you see
how things can be.
It's the spirit of one who won't give up,
the voice that says it can be done,
and the eagerness to make it happen.

Hope is the belief that anything
    is possible,
the emblem of one who believes
that dreams can come true,
and the joyous attitude of going forward
to reach every goal.
Most especially, hope brings out
the winner that lives in your heart.

Barbara J. Hall

Look for the Sunshine

When life seems like a mountain
   that's too hard to climb…
      you will find the strength
         to take just one more step.
When your journey seems just too hard
   to bear…
      you will find the courage
         to face one more day.
When you feel lost and you don't know
   which way to turn…
      let your faith and trust lead the way.
And when it's hard to believe
   that things will ever get better…
      look inside your heart —
         and find hope.

Remember that every storm passes —
and sunshine and brighter days
   always follow the rain.

Jason Blume

The Greatest Success in Life Is to Live Each Day with Joy

Material wealth definitely has its merits —
but it alone cannot provide the riches
of a truly meaningful life.
A truly meaningful life possesses
an inherent sense of
both self and purpose.
It celebrates truth, love, and freedom
and remains forever appreciative
    of its blessings.
It is a life that gives and cares
and makes a difference
    in endless poignant ways.
It leaves the world a far better
    and brighter place
than it would have otherwise been.

People are often looking for ways
to measure the worth of their lives.
The most fortunate among them
    come to realize that
you need not have the finest education
to possess the greatest wisdom
or the biggest bank account
to feel rich beyond measure.
For if you are joyful and share
    your bliss at every turn,
then you walk among
the most successful beings
to ever grace this earth.

Lynn Keachie

Let Go...

2/8/22

If you want to be healthy morally, mentally, and physically, just let go. Let go of the little annoyances of everyday life, the irritations and the petty vexations that cross your path daily. Don't take them up, nurse them, pet them, and brood over them. They are not worthwhile. Let them go!

Learn to let go. As you value health of body and peace of mind, let go — just simply let go!

Author Unknown

Enough

It's a gift, this cloudless November morning
warm enough for you to walk without a jacket
along your favorite path. The rhythmic shushing
of your feet through fallen leaves should be
enough to quiet the mind, so it surprises you
when you catch yourself telling off your boss
for a decade of accumulated injustices,
all the things you've never said circling inside you.

The rising wind pulls you out of it,
and you look up to see a cloud of leaves
wheeling in sunlight, flickering against the blue
and lifting above the treetops, as if the whole day
were sighing, *Let it go, let it go,*
for this moment at least, let it all go.

$\approx$

Jeffrey Harrison

Find Delight in the Little Things

Make a point to delight in every little thing. The more things you consider to be a reason for joy, the more joyful you will be.

A few things are so overwhelmingly positive or so completely negative as to not need any judgment on your part. All the other things, though, depend largely on how you see them.

If you see something as a curse it will be a curse. If you see it as a blessing it will indeed be a blessing for you.

Don't allow others to poison your attitude with their complaints and their gloomy pessimism. Be aggressively and proactively positive.

Find delight in the little things. And you'll be pleasantly surprised at how delightful the big things turn out to be, too.

Ralph Marston

If you want to feel rich, just count all of the things you have that money can't buy.

Author Unknown   1|5|12

Readjust,
Refresh,
Renew,
Remember

Readjust your attitude.
 Start to think positively,
 knowing you have what it takes
 to accomplish your goals.

Refresh your spirit.
 Dream new dreams,
 letting the possibilities
 grow into visions.

Renew your faith.
 Believe you have a purpose —
 a higher calling
 designed just for you.

Remember your loved ones.
 They are there to applaud your victories,
 encourage you on your journey,
 and help you through the challenges.

Sue Davis Potts

Strive for Balance

Imagine life as a game in which you are juggling five balls in the air. You name them — work, family, health, friends, and spirit — and you're keeping all of these in the air. You will soon understand that work is a rubber ball. If you drop it, it will bounce back. But the other four balls — family, health, friends, and spirit are made of glass. If you drop one of these, they will be irrevocably scuffed, marked, nicked, damaged, or even shattered. They will never be the same. You must understand that and strive for balance in your life.

Brian Dyson

Don't just have minutes in the day, have moments in time. Balance out any bad with the good you can provide. Know that you are capable of amazing results. Surprise yourself by discovering new strength inside.

Add a meaningful page to the diary of each day. Do things no one else would even dream of. There is no greater gift than the kind of inner beauty you possess. Do the things you do... with love.

Walk along the pathways that enrich your happiness. Taking care of the "little things" is a big necessity. Don't be afraid of testing your courage. Life is short, but it's long enough to have excitement and serenity.

Don't let the important things go unsaid. Do the things that brighten your life and help you on your way. Live life to the fullest; make each day count.

— Collin McCarty

Surround Yourself
with Positivity

Never allow anyone
to discourage you
from following your dreams.
Surround yourself
with encouraging
and helpful people —
optimists who will get you excited
about your dreams and goals.

Surround yourself
with supportive people —
the ones who tell you
that giving up is crazy
because you are so good
at what you do.

You cannot waste
the passion and talent
you have been blessed with.
Don't allow the negative people
to bring you down...
let the positive ones lift you up.

≈

April Aragam

Seek out that particular mental attribute
which makes you feel most deeply and
vitally alive, along with which comes
the inner voice which says, "This is the
real me," and when you have found that
attitude, follow it.

William James

The purpose of life, after all, is to live it,
to taste experience to the utmost, to reach
out eagerly and without fear for newer and
richer experience.

3/19/22

Eleanor Roosevelt

When all is said and done,
I will judge my life
by the people I met along the way,
the friends I laughed with,
shared with, and cried with;
the people who held me up
when it seemed like
all I could do was fall;
who made me laugh
when there was nothing left to say;
who accepted me
and celebrated me
for being exactly who I am.

Vanessa Bridson

Make Time to Play...

Play is the gateway to vitality. By its nature it is uniquely and intrinsically rewarding. It generates optimism, seeks out novelty, makes perseverance fun, leads to mastery, gives the immune system a bounce, fosters empathy, and promotes a sense of belonging and community.

The National Institute for Play

Find Reasons to Smile

Spend awhile in the garden or the park or the path amongst the trees. Do the things that please you, as well as the things you have to do. Fulfill the work and the tasks of the day while discovering something new and different along the way. Grow, learn, reach out. Be curious. Be childlike.

Remember what imagination is all about. Share a smile, a feeling, a certain personal thought from the heart, from the soul. Care. Kick off your shoes. Sing along with your song. Be less concerned about what others think of you. Be more accepting of the very special person who lives inside you.

Collin McCarty

Laugh Loudly and Often

Make the best of your circumstances. No one has everything, and everyone has something of sorrow intermingled with gladness of life. The trick is to make the laughter outweigh the tears.

Robert Louis Stevenson

A good laugh provides a cathartic release, a cleansing of emotions, and a release of emotional tension. Even after the laughter has ended, body tensions continue to decrease. So the next time you're feeling sad or stressed, flash a big smile or give a hearty laugh. There's a lot of truth in the old adage, "Those who laugh... last."

Joan Lunden

There is one kind of laugh that I always did recommend; it looks out of the eye first with a merry twinkle, then it creeps down on its hands and knees and plays around the mouth like a pretty moth around the blaze of a candle, then it steals over into the dimples of the cheeks and rides around in those whirlpools for a while, then it lights up the whole face like the mellow bloom on a damask rose, then it swims up on the air, with a peal as clear and as happy as a dinner-bell, then it goes back again on gold tiptoes like an angel out for an airing, and it lies down on its little bed of violets in the heart where it came from.

Josh Billings

Find Happiness
in Everything You Do

Find happiness in nature
in the beauty of a mountain
in the serenity of the sea
Find happiness in friendship
in the fun of doing things together
in the sharing and understanding
Find happiness in your family
in the stability of knowing
  that someone cares
in the strength of love and honesty
Find happiness in yourself
in your mind and body
in your values and achievements
Find happiness in
everything
you
do

Susan Polis Schutz

Forgive

Forgiveness is letting go of the pain
and accepting what has happened
because it will not change.

Forgiveness is dismissing the blame.
Choices were made that caused the hurt;
you each could have chosen differently,
but you didn't.

Forgiveness is looking at the pain,
learning the lessons it has produced,
and understanding what you have learned.

Forgiveness allows you to move on
toward a better understanding
of universal love
and your true purpose.

Forgiveness is knowing that love
is the answer to all questions
and that we all
are in some way connected.

Forgiveness is starting over
with the knowledge
that you have gained.
It is saying:
"I forgive you, and I forgive myself.
I hope you can do the same."

Judith Mammay

Celebrate the Sheer Joy
of Being Alive

Just to look at the sun going down behind green hills; just to watch rain falling on a quiet lake; just to see spinning tops of sand, created by winds whirling over a desert; just to be able to imagine oneself upon a ship, docking at a pier in a strange and distant port; just to be able to touch the hand of another and feel oneself become a part of that other; just to breathe the evening air and hear the voices of children, raised in laughter; Oh! just to feel one is a part of all the scheme of things entire — such are the blessings humans have.

G. Allison Phelps

The world is full of miracles for our five senses if we just open ourselves up to receive them. The trick is to look with fresh eyes, hear with new ears. When we do, we come alive again to the wonders all around us — the slant of light on the skyscraper, the smell of hot asphalt as the rain hits the pavement, the sparkle of a stranger's smile — and we feel an uplift of emotion. We touch the sheer joy of being alive.

This uplift is available, free, with no expiration date in every moment of our existence. We can tap into it anywhere, anytime if we but tune into the world around us.

Mary Jane Ryan

Get the Most out of Every Day

Promise yourself...
to follow the path
that best affirms your values,
expresses your passion,
and empowers your soul;
to balance work with play,
learning with teaching,
and words with deeds.

Promise yourself...
to treat people with respect
for their differences
and compassion for their pain;
to appreciate that everyone
has a reason for doing what they do,
feeling how they feel,
and being where they are.
Promise to remember this about others...
and know it about yourself.

Promise yourself...
to say "yes" to your curiosity
and "no" to your fears;
to keep your goals clear in your mind
and close to your heart;
to choose relationships that allow
for the fullest expression of
your interests, feelings, and self —
and to build on those that nourish you;
to be the one who makes things happen
when others make excuses
and the one who gives even more
when others give up.

Promise to put your best
into every task...
and get the most out of every day.

Paula Finn

The Six Most Important Things You Can Do

≈ Look in the mirror and smile... and see an amazing person looking back at you. You really are someone special, and your presence is a present to the world around you.

≈ When you're counting your blessings, be sure to include the privilege of having a new sunrise every morning and a brand-new beginning every day.

≈ Don't ever give up on your hopes and dreams. Your happiness is depending on you to stay strong.

≈ Know that you can reach deep inside and find everything you need to get through each moment that lies ahead.

≈ When you talk to those who matter most, open the door to your heart. The wider it is, the easier it will be for things like compassion and understanding to come inside. And it just naturally follows... the more wonderful visitors you have, the more your life will shine.

≈ Unwind a little and smile a lot and try not to worry too much. Know that you're loved and cared for... and that, whenever you need them, your guardian angels are great about working overtime.

Douglas Pagels

A Positive Attitude
Is at the Heart of All
Happiness and Success

You are made to dream, to hope,
   and to imagine;
you are meant to reach, to stretch,
   and to soar;
you are created to laugh, to live,
   and to love.

There is enough that can go wrong in life
   without undermining yourself.
Life tends to grant you exactly what
   you invite in with your thoughts.
If you think, act, and talk negatively,
   your world will most likely be negative.
Your attitude is a choice you make.

It's possible to change your life
    by simply adjusting your attitude.
Optimism and enthusiasm will most often
    create real achievement and lasting joy.
It takes so little in life to be truly happy,
    and most everything you need
        can be found within yourself —
in your own heart and soul,
    in the way you choose to think.

Get rid of negative thoughts,
    and try to avoid negative people.
Think, act, and talk with honesty,
    integrity, and a positive attitude.
Surround yourself with encouraging,
    loving people, and you will attain
        a deep sense of inner peace,
which is the heart of all happiness
    and true success.

Vickie M. Worsham

You Are
What You Think
You Are

You will be whatever you resolve to be.
Determine to be something in the world,
and you will be something.

"I cannot," never accomplished anything.

But "I will try," has worked wonders.

≈

Joel Hawes

Everything can be taken from a man but
one thing: the last of the human freedoms —
to choose one's attitude in any given set of
circumstances, to choose one's own way.

≈

Viktor E. Frankl

Count Your Blessings

If we knew how much the habit of being thankful might do for us, I am sure we would take time out every day to count up a few of our blessings. When the spirit of thankfulness takes its place in our consciousness, we radiate life from the very center of our being to the world about us.

≈

Author Unknown

The happiest people in the world are those who have a hard time recalling their worries... and an easy time remembering their blessings.

≈

Alin Austin

Gratitude unlocks the fullness of life. Gratitude makes things right. It turns what we have into enough, and more. It turns denial into acceptance, chaos to order, confusion to clarity. It can turn a meal into a feast, a house into a home, a stranger into a friend. It turns problems into gifts, failures into successes, the unexpected into perfect timing, and mistakes into important events. It can turn an existence into a real life, and disconnected situations into important and beneficial lessons. Gratitude makes sense of our past, brings peace for today, and creates a vision for tomorrow.

Melody Beattie

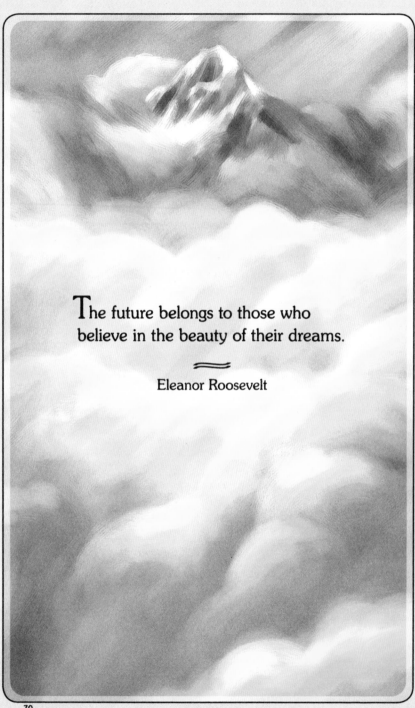

The future belongs to those who
believe in the beauty of their dreams.

Eleanor Roosevelt

Don't Be Afraid to Dream

Remember that a wish
can take you anywhere —
and half the fun is reaching for a star.
Your dreams were made to soar;
let your spirit dance
in every waking moment.
Every day comes bearing gifts;
hold each promise in your hands.
Within you is your very own universe.
A bit of stardust is blowing your way —
a bit of light and a bit of wonder.
Follow your leanings;
listen to the whispers of your soul.

Linda E. Knight

Your Life Can Be Whatever You Want It to Be

Knowing in your heart that you are in charge of your destiny can give you the power to overcome obstacles. It's an attitude that carries you through the tough times and that looks at the positives and defies the negatives.

≈

Barbara Cage

We are haunted by an ideal life, and it is because we have within us the beginning and the possibility of it.

≈

Phillips Brooks

I think that if you just follow your heart… you can do anything. You can have anything possible. That's what I've experienced….

We all have the ability to do whatever we set out to do. You just find the ways; you just create the opportunities.

Cameron Diaz

It is never too late to be what you might have been.

George Eliot

Practice Optimism

Meet each challenge
with strength and courage.
Listen to your heart,
find wisdom to take the right path,
and show your strength and courage
by being patient.
Stand up
for what you believe in,
say "no" to that which is not
compatible with your values,
and show your strength and courage
by being true to yourself.

Open new doors for yourself
even when you seem too tired to go on.
Find the energy to see a new dawn —
a new point of view —
and create a new direction
where none seems possible.
Show your strength and courage
by being optimistic.

Bonnie St. John

Refuse to Be Unhappy

Refuse to let your troubles multiply;
    just take them one by one.
Organize your time; keep your life simple
    and exactly the way you want it.
Refuse to complain about things;
    learn to improve your surroundings
and create your world
    the way you believe it should be.
Refuse to dwell on the mistakes
    or disappointments
that are sometimes a part of life;
instead learn how you can
    make things better.

Be energetic and positive
    about the things you do,
and always hope for the best.
Believe in yourself at all times
    and in all aspects of your life.
Before you know it,
those wonderful dreams
you have believed in all your life
    will come true,
and your life will be
the happy and successful life
    that it was meant to be.

Ben Daniels

At Least Once
Every Day...

Treat yourself to something
that makes you happy.
Give yourself permission
to be wrong.
Applaud yourself for
the smallest success;
forgive yourself for
the greatest defeat.
Appreciate yourself
for the effort you made,
the good you did,
and the joy you shared.

Accept yourself for
what you are,
for what you are…
is beautiful.

Paula Finn

Believe in the
Power of You

When things get to be too much and it seems like there are no alternatives or solutions, believe you can overcome the adversities facing you and know that things will eventually improve.

Life carries doubts and uncertainties. There are no guarantees and certainly no crystal balls. Yet there is always hope. There is kindness and caring from others. There is the assurance of love, which will always be a safeguard and security. Believe in the power of positive energy in your life.

Believe in the power of You.

Debbie Burton-Peddle

This life is yours
Take the power
to choose what you want to do
and do it well
Take the power
to love what you want in life
and love it honestly
Take the power
to walk in the forest
and be a part of nature
Take the power
to control your own life
No one else can do it for you
Take the power
to make your life
healthy
exciting
worthwhile
and very happy

Susan Polis Schutz

Start Today,
and Make It a Habit

You have a chance to be as happy as any one person has ever been. You have an opportunity to be as proud as anyone you've ever known. You have the potential to make a very special dream come true.

And all you have to do... is recognize the possibilities, the power, and the wonder of... today.

— Douglas Pagels

Positive thinking is a habit, like any other; we can practice it every day until it becomes second nature to us — and along the way, transform our lives.

— Washington L. Crowley

May Every Dawn Bring...

Dreams that are always
deep enough to bless you,
strong enough to guide you,
and big enough to take you
to the stars and beyond;
small pleasures and big joys
and happy skies that always
shine down upon you;
more smiles and laughter
than you have ever had before;
contentment and well-being
that follow you everywhere;
all the things that mean
the world to you;
prayers that soar to heaven;
and a guardian angel at your side.

May every dawn be a place
full of beauty and happy endings.
May you feel glad in your heart,
    joyous in your spirit,
        and grateful for your life.

Linda E. Knight

You Can Do It!

You can be optimistic. Because people who expect things to turn out for the best often set the stage to receive a beautiful result.

You can put things in perspective. Because some things are important, and others are definitely not.

You can remember that beyond the clouds, the sun is still shining. You can meet each challenge and give it all you've got.

You can count your blessings. You can be inspired to climb your ladders and have some nice, long talks with your wishing stars. You can be strong and patient. You can be gentle and wise.

And you can believe in happy endings. Because you are the author of the story of your life.

Douglas Pagels

Let These Words
Be Your Guide

As long as you keep trying you won't ever stop achieving. Keep feeding your mind, and it won't go hungry for ideas. Stay optimistic, and you won't ever lose hope.

Embrace change, and you'll keep on growing forever. Keep making new friends, and your circle will constantly expand. Nurture the talents of others, and you'll always get results.

Be a promise keeper, and you'll keep people's trust. Be who you are, and you'll always be real. Give credit to those who helped you reach goals, and you'll always have a team.

Keep aiming high, and you'll always have dreams. Keep your eyes open, and you'll see opportunities. Keep your enthusiasm, and you'll always be inspired.

Be patient and persistent, and you won't ever feel the need to quit. Seek help when you need it, and you'll never struggle alone.

Keep your energy, passion, and excitement for life, and you'll never be bored or discontented. Stay focused on your goals and not on who others want you to be or what they want you to achieve.

When making decisions, listen to your logical mind, but don't leave behind the wisdom of your instincts and the messages from your heart. Listen to all of them, and do what's right for you. Let your faith be a guiding light and daily comfort, and you will always feel blessed.

Let these words be your guide to a positive life. Keep them in your mind, heart, and spirit. Use them, and the guiding principles you discover on your own, to create for yourself the future you choose.

— Jacqueline Schiff

May You Always Have Positive Thoughts

May the days be good to you: comforting more often than crazy and giving more often than taking.

May the passing seasons make sure that any heartaches are replaced with a million smiles and that any hard journeys eventually turn into nice, easy miles that take you everywhere you want to go.

May your dreams do their absolute best to
   come true.
May your heart be filled with the kindness
   of friends, the caring of everyone you love,
   and the richness of memories you wouldn't
   trade for anything.

May life's little worries always stay small.
May you get a little closer every day to any goals
   you want to achieve.

May any changes be good ones and any challenges
   turn out to be for the better.

May you find time to do the things you've always
   wanted to do!

And may you have positive thoughts forever.

Douglas Pagels

Acknowledgments

We gratefully acknowledge the permission granted by the following authors, publishers, and authors' representatives to reprint poems or excerpts from their publications.

PrimaDonna Entertainment Corp. for "Don't Let Anything Steal Your Joy" and "You've Got Choices" by Donna Fargo. Copyright © 2005, 2010 by PrimaDonna Entertainment Corp. All rights reserved.

Barbara J. Hall for "You Don't Have to Accept Defeat" and "As Long as You Have Hope, All Things Are Possible." Copyright © 2011 by Barbara J. Hall. All rights reserved.

Lynn Keachie for "We Can't Control the Outer World, but We Can Master the One Within," "You Can Rise Above Anything," and "The Greatest Success in Life Is to Live Each Day with Joy." Copyright © 2011 by Lynn Keachie. All rights reserved.

Angela Rene Goughnour for "Keep Moving Forward." Copyright © 2011 by Angela Rene Goughnour. All rights reserved.

Christina Curtis for "Try Not to Worry." Copyright © 2011 by Christina Curtis. All rights reserved.

Broadway Books, a division of Random House, Inc., for "Setbacks and disappointments are…" from MARY LOU RETTON'S GATEWAYS TO HAPPINESS by Mary Lou Retton. Copyright © 2000 by MLR Entertainment, Inc. and Momentum Partners, Inc. All rights reserved. And for "The world is full of miracles…" from THE HAPPINESS MAKEOVER by Mary Jane Ryan. Copyright © 2005 by Mary Jane Ryan. All rights reserved.

Jason Blume for "Look for the Sunshine." Copyright © 2008 by Jason Blume. All rights reserved.

Jeffrey Harrison, www.jeffreyharrisonpoet.com, for "Enough" from "Poem-a-Day," published by the Academy of American Poets, www.poets.org. Copyright © 2010 by Jeffrey Harrison. Reprinted by permission. All rights reserved.

"The Daily Motivator," www.dailymotivator.com, for "Find Delight in the Little Things" by Ralph Marston, Jr. Copyright © 2003 by Ralph Marston, Jr. Reprinted by permission. All rights reserved.

Sue Davis Potts for "Readjust, Refresh, Renew, Remember." Copyright © 2011 by Sue Davis Potts. All rights reserved.

Brian Dyson for "Imagine life as a game…." Copyright © 1991 by Brian Dyson. All rights reserved.

April Aragam for "Surround Yourself with Positivity." Copyright © 2011 by April Aragam. All rights reserved.

Vanessa Bridson for "When all is said and done…." Copyright © 2011 by Vanessa Bridson. All rights reserved.

The National Institute for Play, www.nifplay.org, for "Play is the gateway…" from "Personal Health and Well-Being." Copyright © 2008 by the National Institute for Play. All rights reserved.

Joan Lunden Productions, www.joanlunden.com, for "A good laugh provides…" from WAKE-UP CALLS: MAKING THE MOST OF EVERY DAY by Joan Lunden. Copyright © 2001 by New Life Entertainment, Inc. All rights reserved.

Paula Finn for "Get the Most out of Every Day" and "At Least Once Every Day…." Copyright © 2011 by Paula Finn. All rights reserved.

Vickie M. Worsham for "A Positive Attitude Is at the Heart of All Happiness and Success." Copyright © 2011 by Vickie M. Worsham. All rights reserved.

Beacon Press for "Everything can be taken…" from MAN'S SEARCH FOR MEANING by Viktor E. Frankl. Copyright © 1959, 1962, 1984, 1992, 2006 by Viktor E. Frankl. All rights reserved.

Melody Beattie and Hazelden Publishing for "Gratitude unlocks the fullness of life" from GRATITUDE by Melody Beattie. Copyright © 1992 by Melody Beattie. All rights reserved.

Marianne Schnall for "I think that if you just follow…" by Cameron Diaz from DARING TO BE OURSELVES. Copyright © 2010 by Marianne Schnall. All rights reserved.

Debbie Burton-Peddle for "When things get to be too much…." Copyright © 2011 by Debbie Burton-Peddle. All rights reserved.

Jacqueline Schiff for "Let These Words Be Your Guide…." Copyright © 2011 by Jacqueline Schiff. All rights reserved.

A careful effort has been made to trace the ownership of poems used in this anthology in order to obtain permission to reprint copyrighted materials and give proper credit to the copyright owners. If any error or omission has occurred, it is completely inadvertent, and we would like to make corrections in future editions provided that written notification is made to the publisher:

BLUE MOUNTAIN ARTS, INC., P.O. Box 4549, Boulder, Colorado 80306.